W9-CFJ-410

Unsolved Mysteries

Amazing
Predictions

Brian Innes

RSVP

**RAINTREE
STECK-VAUGHN**
PUBLISHERS
A Steck-Vaughn Company

Austin, Texas

Developed by Brown Partworks
Editor: Lindsey Lowe
Designer: Joan Curtis

Raintree Steck-Vaughn Publishers Staff
Project Manager: Joyce Spicer
Editor: Pam Wells

Library of Congress Cataloging-in-Publication Data
Innes, Brian.
　　Amazing predictions/by Brian Innes.
　　　　p.　　cm.—(Unsolved mysteries)
　　Includes bibliographical references and index.
　　Summary: Describes predictions people have made that came true,
including a 1979 airplane disaster, President Lincoln's dream of his own
assassination, and the sinking of the *Titanic*.
　　ISBN 0-8172-5480-3 (Hardcover)
　　ISBN 0-8172-4277-5 (Softcover)
　　1. Prophecies (Occultism)—History—Juvenile literature.
[1. Prophecies.] I. Title. II. Series: Innes, Brian. Unsolved mysteries.
BF1791.I56　1999
133.3—dc21　　　　　　　　　　　　　　98-10071
　　　　　　　　　　　　　　　　　　　　CIP
　　　　　　　　　　　　　　　　　　　　AC

Printed and bound in the United States
1 2 3 4 5 6 7 8 9 0　WZ　02 01 00 99 98

Acknowledgments

Cover Ellen Schuster/The Image Bank;
Page 5: Hulton Getty; **Page 7:** John H. Clark/Corbis;
Page 9: Corbis-Bettmann; **Page 10:** Popperfoto;
Page 11: Robert Estall/Corbis; **Page 13:** Topham
Picturepoint; **Page 14:** Popperfoto; **Page 15:** Hulton
Getty; **Page 16:** Leonard de Selva/Corbis;
Page 19: Jean-Loup Charmet; **Page 20:** ET Archive;
Page 22: Gianni Dagli Orti; **Page 23:** Library of
Congress/Corbis; **Pages 24 and 25:** Corbis-
Bettmann; **Page 27:** Topham Picturepoint;
Page 28: Hulton Getty; **Page 30:** Michael
Nicholson/Corbis; **Page 31:** AKG, London;
Page 32: Charles Walker Collection/Images Colour
Library; **Page 33:** Ronald Reagan Library/Corbis;
Page 35: Charles Walker Collection/Images Colour
Library; **Page 37:** Mary Evans Picture Library;
Page 39: NASA/Corbis; **Page 41:** Kobal Collection.
Page 43: NASA/Corbis; **Page 44:** Topham
Picturepoint; **Page 45:** Ronald Reagan
Library/Corbis; **Page 46:** Richard Smith/Corbis.

Contents

A Dream Come True   4

Visions of Terror   12

Words of Prophecy   18

All in the Stars   26

The Hand of Fate   34

Predictions in Literature   38

Can We See the Future?   42

Glossary   47

Index   48

Further Reading   48

A Dream Come True

Many people's dreams do come true. But they have not always brought fortune and fame. Some have warned of disaster.

On the night of March 8, 1946, John Godley, a young Irishman, had a dream. He dreamed he saw the next day's newspaper. The page he glimpsed gave the horse racing results.

When he woke, he could remember the names of two horses on the page—"Bindal" and "Juladin." Both had won their races. He looked in the morning newspaper, and sure enough, a horse named Bindal was racing that afternoon. A horse named Juladin was racing at another event.

Excited, Godley bet money on each of the horses. They both won. The chances of both horses racing on the same afternoon and both winning were less than one in 1,000.

A WINNING STREAK

On April 4, Godley was at his home in Ireland. Again he dreamed that he was looking at a list of race winners. The only name he remembered was "Tubermore." He discovered that there was a horse called "Tuberose" racing the next day at Aintree, Liverpool. John Godley, his family, and friends, bet money on the horse—and Tuberose won.

"In 1958 Godley had a final success. He dreamed that a horse named 'What Man?' won Britain's most famous race. . . ."

Godley continued to have winning dreams. On one occasion he bet on two horses. He wrote out a statement of his predictions and had it witnessed by three friends. He took it to the nearest post office, where the postmaster stamped it with his official time stamp, and sealed it in an envelope.

Both horses won, and Godley became famous. A British newspaper published an article about him. Soon afterward they offered him a job as horse racing correspondent. People wrote to him from all over the world asking him his secret.

SWEET DREAMS

In 1958 Godley had a final success. He dreamed that a horse named "What Man?" won Britain's most famous race, the Grand National. A horse named "Mr. What" was racing. Godley bet on it—and won a large sum of money.

Some people would say Godley's was a trivial gift. Predicting the result of a horse race is not very important—except to the person who dreams it! But Godley's story is unusual. Most dreams that predict the future don't keep happening over such a long period of time.

A VIVID VISION

David Booth was an office manager in Cincinnati, Ohio. In May 1979 he had the same dream ten nights in a row. The dream was startlingly real. "It was like I was standing there, watching the whole thing—like watching television." He heard an airliner's engines failing. Then he saw a big three-engine jet with American Airlines markings. It swerved, rolled over, and crashed to the ground.

Each night he woke in horror, the sound of the explosion ringing in his ears. He could even feel the intense heat of the flames.

Terrified, Booth called American Airlines on May 22. He also called the Federal Aviation Administration (FAA). He even told a psychiatrist at Cincinnati University. Everybody pointed out there was nothing they could do. They needed more information before they could act.

On the sunny afternoon of May 25, three days later, an American Airlines DC-10 took off from O'Hare International Airport, Chicago. The plane just lifted off the ground. Then, the left engine and part of the wing broke off. The plane climbed to 350 feet (105 m). It turned over and crashed in a huge ball of flame. Two hundred and fifty-eight passengers, 13 crew, and two people on the ground were killed instantly.

It happened just as David Booth had seen in his dream ten nights in a row. The American Airlines DC-10 took off on a fine afternoon from Chicago's O'Hare International Airport. Seconds later the plane rolled over and crashed to the ground.

A spokesman for the FAA described Booth's dreams as "uncanny." The similarities were remarkable. The airline was named; the plane had three jet engines; it rolled over. The FAA claimed they had tried to match the dreams with known airports and airplanes. But it was not until the crash actually occurred that the details fell into place.

Terrible disasters such as this often seem to be foreseen in dreams. They appear more often than other happenings. This is because the dreams are so clear and horrifying that people remember them when they wake.

DOOMED LEADER

President Abraham Lincoln had a vivid dream one April night in 1865. He dreamed he was wakened by sobbing. He got up and went to see what it was. In the East Room of the White House, soldiers were guarding a body lying in state. People were filing past a coffin.

"It's the President. He was killed by an assassin."

LINCOLN'S DREAM

Lincoln could not see the face of the dead person. He asked one of the soldiers who it was. "It's the President," replied the guard. "He was killed by an assassin." There was a cry of grief from the mourners so loud it woke Lincoln.

President Lincoln told his wife, Mary, about the dream. He also told several friends. A few days later, on April 14, in Ford's Theater, Washington, D.C.,

President Lincoln had foreseen his own assassination in a dream. But the dream did not tell him where or when the assassination would occur. So he went to the Ford's Theater in Washington, D.C., on the night of April 14, 1865, as planned.

Lincoln was shot by actor John Wilkes Booth. The President died the following day.

DREAMING OF DISASTER

In 1947 a group of British doctors and psychiatrists agreed to keep a record of their dreams. The dreams would be reported in letters. They found that more than one member of the group was likely to have a dream about a future event. Added together, the dreams could give a powerful indication of what might happen.

On the nights of September 2 and 3, 1954, psychiatrist Dr. Alice Buck dreamed of an air disaster.

9

The time of 3:00 A.M. seemed to be particularly important. During the night of September 3, one of the other members of the group dreamed of men and women struggling on a journey. They were overwhelmed by water.

Early on September 4 a KLM Constellation airliner crashed close to Shannon Airport, in the west of Ireland. One daily newspaper reported: "Men and women died yesterday, trapped in darkness in the cabin of a crashed airliner slowly filling with the muddy waters of the Shannon River. One man had clung for three hours to the tail of the almost submerged airliner, waiting for rescue. The plane crashed at 3:40 A.M."

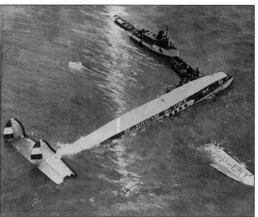

Two dreamers predicted the crash of this KLM Constellation airliner. It crashed into the waters of the Shannon River in Ireland early in the morning of September 4, 1954. Of the 56 on board, 27 died and 29 were rescued.

In 1902 an aircraft designer named John William Dunne dreamed of a volcano on an island erupting. In his dream it killed 40,000 people. Not long afterward Mount Pelée in Martinique erupted—with a death toll of 40,000.

In the fall of 1913, Dunne told his sister of another dream. He had dreamed of a train that had fallen over an embankment, just north of the Forth Bridge in Scotland. On April 14, 1914, the famous train named *The Flying Scotsman* was derailed 15 miles (24 km) north of the Forth Bridge. It plunged nearly 20 feet (6 m) onto the golf course below. Dunne kept a record of more than 20 dreams of this kind.

DREAMING OF RICHES

A much happier dream is still remembered in the town of Swaffham, in Norfolk, England, more than 500 years after it happened.

In the 15th century, John Chapman was a peddler in Swaffham. In a dream, he was told to go to London and wait on London Bridge. It took Chapman more than three days to walk the 100 miles (160 km) to London. Once there, he waited on the bridge. Finally, after three days, he decided he had wasted his time. So he turned to walk home.

Just then, a man asked Chapman what he had been waiting for. Chapman told him about the dream, without telling his name. The man laughed. "If I believed in dreams, I'd be as great a fool as you. Not long ago, I dreamed about a place called Swaffham. A peddler named John Chapman lives there. I dreamed that a pot of money is buried under a tree in his garden. Just think, if I'd traveled all that way to dig for it, because of a dream—what a fool I'd be!" Hearing this, Chapman went home.

He found the money under the tree and used some of it to help build a new church. The full story of what happened is told in the church's stained-glass windows.

This memorial in the town of Swaffham, England, shows: "Ye Pedlar of Swaffham who did by a dream find great treasure."

Visions of Terror

Many people have predicted tragedies and disasters days, months, even years before they occurred.

On the morning of October 21, 1966, classes had just assembled in Pantglas Junior School. It was in the little village of Aberfan, Wales. At 9:15 A.M. a huge, two-million ton mound of wet coal-mining waste, the slag heap, slid down from a mountain above the school and buried it. A black avalanche poured through the classrooms. It smashed through a row of houses across the street. A total of 144 people died. Of these, 116 were schoolchildren.

One was 10-year-old Eryl Mai Jones. Two weeks before the tragedy, she said to her mother, "I'm not afraid to die." Megan Jones remarked that she was too young to talk of dying. "But I shall be with my friends, Peter and June," Eryl replied. On October 20 she told her mother about a dream she had. "I went to school, and there was no school there. Something black had come down all over it."

Next morning, Eryl went off to Pantglas School, as usual. Her body was eventually dug out of the mound of black waste. It was laid to rest with the bodies of the other victims of the disaster in a communal grave. Eryl's body was placed between those of Peter and June.

Eryl Mai Jones was buried in a mass grave (opposite) with her classmates.

12

"I'm not afraid to die . . . I went to school, and there was no school there. . . ."

ERYL MAI JONES

One of those who visited the site next day was psychiatrist Dr. J. C. Barker. He heard the story and wondered whether anybody else had had a premonition of the disaster. At his request, the London *Evening Standard* newspaper then published an appeal. It asked anyone who had experienced any forewarning of the tragedy to write in.

SHARED HORROR

In all, some 200 people wrote to the newspaper claiming to have had visions, or feelings, of a disaster about to happen. Dr. Barker himself received 76 letters. He

On October 21, 1966, two million tons of coal-mining waste slid down a mountain onto an elementary school in Aberfan, Wales. Pupil Eryl Mai Jones foresaw "something black had come down all over it."

came to the conclusion that at least 60 were genuine. In 24 cases Dr. Barker was able to confirm that the details had been told to others before the event.

Mrs. Grace Engleton was one of these cases. She wrote from Sidcup, Kent, more than 300 miles (480 km) away from Aberfan. "I have never been to Wales. Nor do I possess a television set. On the night of October 14, I had a vivid, horrible dream of a terrible disaster in a coal-mining village. It was in a valley, with a big building filled with young children. Mountains of coal and water were rushing down upon the valley, burying the building. The screams of those children were so vivid that I screamed myself."

Her neighbor confirmed that Mrs. Engleton had told her about the dream on October 17—four days before the event. Other people reported having premonitions of a coming disaster several weeks—or even months—before the events at Aberfan. Several men and women developed symptoms of acute mental and physical unease. Others reported dreams or visions of screaming children. Some saw falling mountains and black mud. In three cases people named the village, or something close to it.

Premonitions like this have occurred throughout history. Before the 19th century they were thought to be communicated by "spirits." Such spirits were said to be angelic or devilish. Only those brave enough to suffer criticism, or even persecution, admitted to having these thoughts. With the increase in general education, however, and the development of science, premonitions began to be studied.

Stunned Londoners react to news of the Titanic disaster. Many people had vivid forewarnings of the terrible fate that awaited the "unsinkable" new liner. An English woman watching the mighty ship depart suddenly screamed out: "You fools, I can see hundreds of people struggling in the icy water."

THE SINKING OF THE *TITANIC*

Some of the best documented cases of premonitions concern the sinking of the British liner *Titanic* on her maiden voyage. The ship struck an iceberg on the night of April 14, 1912. About 1,500 of the 2,207 people aboard lost their lives.

On March 23, Mr. J. C. Middleton booked a passage to New York on the liner. A week later, he dreamed that "I saw her floating on the sea,

15

keel upward with her passengers and crew swimming around her." He was relieved to receive a cable telling him to delay his sailing.

Joan Grant described watching the *Titanic* leave England on her maiden voyage. She was standing with her parents. Suddenly, her mother cried out, "That ship is going to sink before she reaches America. . . . Do something! You fools, I can see hundreds of people struggling in the icy water!"

The journalist W. T. Stead wrote about the sinking of a great liner. On June 21, 1911, he received

The New White Star Liner,
R.M.S. "TITANIC"

TITANIC

provides for her first-class passengers
VINOLIA OTTO TOILET SOAP
the highest standard of Toilet Luxury and comfort at sea.

VINOLIA COMPANY LTD.,   LONDON AND PARIS.

The prestige of the new White Star flagship Titanic *was so great that advertisers rushed to identify themselves with her even before her maiden voyage. The makers of Vinolia Otto soap clearly had no premonition of the disaster that was to happen on the night of April 14, 1912.*

a letter from a palmist called Cheiro. Cheiro wrote: "Any danger of violent death to you must be by water. . . . Very dangerous for you should be April 1912, especially about the middle of the month. So don't travel by water then if you can help it."

"That ship is going to sink before she reaches America. . . . Do something!. . ."

DOCKSIDE SPECTATOR

Soon afterward, psychic W. de Kerlor told Stead that he would travel to America. De Kerlor warned him: "I dreamed that I was in the midst of a catastrophe on the water; there were masses of bodies struggling in the water. . . ." In spite of these warnings Stead sailed on the *Titanic*—to his death.

The most remarkable premonition of the *Titanic* tragedy appeared in a novel called *Futility*. This was written by Morgan Robertson in 1898. In it, he described the building of a great ocean liner, named *Titan*. During an April voyage she struck an iceberg and sank. There was terrible loss of life. Robertson gave technical details of the liner, and the number of passengers involved. They were remarkably close to those of the *Titanic*.

In all these cases the people involved were aware of their premonitions. Other people may not be conscious of their premonitions. They might have a dream and forget it when they wake. Their premonition can still affect their future actions—even though they are not aware of its influence.

Words of Prophecy

People have made prophecies throughout history. Many of these have come true with chilling accuracy.

The word "prophecy" comes from old Greek. It means "speaking before." In ancient times a prophet was someone who spoke messages. They were believed to be from a god or from gods. There have been hundreds of prophecies made over the centuries. But most have been difficult to interpret.

THE WRITINGS OF NOSTRADAMUS

Michel de Nostredame, known as Nostradamus, was born in Provence, southern France, in 1503. He studied medicine and astrology. Between 1555 and 1558 he published a book called *Centuries*. *Centuries* is a collection of four-line verses—"quatrains"—written in a strange mixture of old French, Italian, Greek, and Latin. There are puns, anagrams, and all sorts of symbolic code words. The quatrains are gathered into groups of about 100 verses, which Nostradamus called the "centuries."

The verses are difficult to understand. Nostradamus said he had written these verses "in a cloudy manner, so as not to upset my readers." They are not in any logical order. One of these quatrains made Nostradamus

Many people believe that Michel de Nostredame—known as Nostradamus—(opposite) predicted the atomic bomb and AIDS.

". . . prophecies of the Great Fire of London, the rise of Napoleon, and the two World Wars of the 20th century."

famous within four years, however. It is one of the easiest to understand:

> *The young lion overcomes the old.*
> *On field of combat, in a single fight,*
> *He will pierce his eyes in a cage of gold.*
> *Two death bells, one, then dying, cruel death.*

The French queen, Catherine de Médicis, heard of this prophecy. She feared it referred to her husband, King Henri II. She summoned Nostradamus to the court in Paris in August 1556, and talked with him.

Three years later, in 1559, a series of tournaments was held in Paris. Henri rode against Gabriel de Lorges, the captain of the Scottish Guard. The two

In 1559, Henri II of France was mortally wounded during a tournament to celebrate the marriage of Philip II of Spain. Henri's wife Catherine de Médicis had heard of Nostradamus's prophecy, and Nostradamus's reputation was made.

men held their lances horizontal. They rode their horses straight toward each other. Twice they both missed. The third time, the lance of de Lorges broke. The splintered point entered through the visor, the movable eye shield, of Henri's helmet. It pierced his eye and brain. He died ten days later in agony.

"You, Madame la Duchesse, and many other ladies, will be taken to the scaffold. . . ."

JACQUES CAZOTTE

Nostradamus's reputation was secured. He died on July 2, 1566. There were still hundreds of quatrains that had not been interpreted. Ever since, people have searched for their meaning. They have found prophecies of the Great Fire of London, the rise of Napoleon, and the two World Wars of the 20th century. They have found predictions of the atomic bomb, the Arab-Israeli conflicts, even the outbreak of AIDS. But no two readers can agree on the meaning of many of the verses.

DEADLY PREDICTIONS

Another man who made a startling prediction was the French writer Jacques Cazotte. His words stunned his fellow guests at a high society dinner in Paris in 1788.

Cazotte announced: "You will see, every one of you, the great revolution for which you are so eager. You know, I am something of a prophet, and I assure you, you shall all see it."

21

As the guests laughed, he continued speaking: "You, Monsieur de Concourt, will die prone on the stone floor of a prison cell. You will perish of a poison you have taken to cheat the executioner. And you, Monsieur de Champfort, will cut your veins 22 times with a razor, and still you will not die—until some months later. As for you, Monsieur de Nicolai, you will die on the scaffold.

"You, Madame la Duchesse, and many other ladies, will be taken to the scaffold in the executioner's cart, with your hands tied behind your back, like common criminals." And, following the French Revolution of 1789, Cazotte's prophecy was fulfilled with chilling accuracy.

On October 16, 1793, the queen of France, Marie Antoinette, died on the guillotine. At a dinner party in 1788, the writer Jacques Cazotte had predicted her gruesome end. This was a year before the outbreak of the French Revolution.

There is no clear difference between prediction and prophecy. Prediction is usually about a specific person, however. It describes specific events that will happen to them.

WARNING OF WAR

A few days after World War I broke out in August 1914, German forces captured a French soldier. What he told them seemed to be impossible. One of the German soldiers was from Bavaria. He was called Andreas Rill. He later wrote a letter to his family all about the French prisoner's prophecies.

The first thing the Frenchman had said was that the Germans should throw away

Burning worthless money in Germany in 1923, during the great inflation—as predicted by a French soldier in 1914.

their guns. They were going to be defeated in the fifth year of the war. Then there would be revolutions in Germany. Everybody would be a millionaire. But they would throw their money from their windows—and nobody would pick it up.

In 1932, a man would come "from the lower ranks" to rule Germany. He would start a new war. This war would begin in 1939. In 1945 Germany would be crushed from all sides. It would become

23

divided. The man and his symbol would disappear. During this time, the German people would suffer.

The letters written by Rill have been examined by the Bavarian State Criminal Police and were found to be genuine. The Frenchman's prophecy came true in every detail. Germany surrendered in November 1918. There were workers' revolts in Germany. Then came several years of runaway inflation. Banknotes were printed for millions of German marks. But the value of the mark was almost nothing. By 1923, one U.S. dollar would buy 4,200 billion marks.

Nazi leader Adolf Hitler had been a corporal in the German army. After the elections in 1932, he rose to become Chancellor of Germany. World War II began in 1939. The destruction in Germany in 1944–45 was terrible. Hitler committed suicide. In the end, his symbol—the swastika—was banned, and Germany was divided in two.

The captured French soldier had one last prophecy. He said there would be a third world war before the year 2000. China would be involved.

PROPHET IN THE UNITED STATES

The most famous modern prophet in the U.S. was Jeane Dixon. She was born Jeane Pickert in 1918, in Wisconsin. As a child she made a number of surprising predictions. When she grew up, she married and moved to Washington, D.C.

By 1956 Jeane Dixon was famous for her prophecies. She claimed she had told Harry S Truman, during World War II,

American psychic Jeane Dixon, who predicted the assassination of Indian leader Mahatma Gandhi.

Jeane Dixon also predicted the death of a young President four years before John F. Kennedy was elected to office. He died in Dallas, Texas, in 1963.

that he would become President. She also predicted the assassination of Indian leader Mahatma Gandhi in 1948.

In May 1956, *Parade* magazine reported that Jeane Dixon had correctly forecast the result of all the presidential elections since 1948. The article continued: "As for the 1960 election, Mrs. Dixon thinks it will be dominated by labor and won by a Democrat. But he will be assassinated, or murdered, or die in office." The knowledge had come to Jeane one morning in the fall of 1952. She was praying in Washington's St. Matthew's Cathedral. She said later:

"Suddenly the White House appeared before me in dazzling brightness. Coming out of a haze, the numerals 1-9-6-0 formed above the roof. An ominous [foretelling disaster, or evil] dark cloud appeared, covering the numbers, and dripped slowly onto the White House. Then I . . . saw a young man, tall and blue-eyed, . . . I was still staring at him when a voice came out of nowhere, telling me that this young man, a Democrat, to be elected as president in 1960, would be assassinated, while in office. The vision . . . stayed with me until that day in Dallas. . . ."

Eleven years later President John F. Kennedy was assassinated on November 22, 1963. His funeral Mass was held in St. Matthew's Cathedral.

All in the Stars

Throughout the ages, people have looked to the stars in order to predict the future.

Astrology is the study of the movement of the planets. It was the first science of the ancient world. It was the science that led to astronomy.

More than 3,000 years ago, priests watched the night sky with awe. They believed that as the Sun, Moon, and the other planets moved about the heavens, they affected events on Earth. The priests thought it was possible to predict coming events by observing these movements. In this way, astrology was born.

Experts who read an astrological chart claim to be able to predict any person's future. Some of the most famous people in history have been the subject of astrological predictions.

HITLER'S HOROSCOPE

Elsbeth Ebertin was born in Görlitz, Germany, on May 14, 1880. As a young woman, she practiced as a professional graphologist—a person who interprets people's characters from their handwriting. In later life she became interested in astrology.

In 1923, a woman sent Ebertin the birth date of Adolf Hitler. She wanted to know Hitler's horoscope. At that time Hitler was attracting

The zodiac (opposite) is divided into 12 groups of stars, or constellations. Early astrologers saw animals, mythical people, and other objects in these groups of stars.

"In the Middle Ages, and later, even scientists believed that astrology could predict events to come."

a lot of attention in Munich because of his new Nazi party. Frau Ebertin published the horoscope in July 1923. She did not reveal whose it was. But she wrote, "A man of action, born on April 20, 1889, with [the] Sun in 29° Aries at the time of his birth, can expose himself to personal danger by . . . uncautious action. He could very likely trigger off an uncontrollable crisis. This man is to be taken very seriously indeed.

Elsbeth Ebertin published Hitler's horoscope in 1923. It was eerily accurate. She said that he was to be taken very seriously indeed, and that he was "destined to play a 'Führer-role' in future battles."

"He is destined to play a 'Führer-role' [a leader's role] in future battles. It seems that the man I have in mind is destined to sacrifice himself for the German nation. He will give an impulse, which will burst forth quite suddenly, to a German freedom movement."

Hitler did indeed trigger a crisis. The world was plunged into World War II as a result. However, he failed to bring Germany freedom or the glorious future that he had planned.

People talk about the "influence of the stars." But in fact, astrology is actually only concerned with the

"A man of action . . . [who] could very likely trigger off an uncontrollable crisis."

ELSBETH EBERTIN ON ADOLF HITLER

movements of the planets, including the Sun and the Moon. They seem to move around against the fixed background of the stars.

Astrologers are interested in the positions of the planets in the sky and their positions relative to one another. They believe this has an influence on people's characters or personalities. This influence is strongest at the moment of birth. To calculate this influence, astrologers draw up a "horoscope." A horoscope is a chart that shows the position of each planet at a particular time.

THE CONSTELLATIONS

The different groups of stars—"constellations"— have special names. These names were given to them many centuries ago. Early astrologers interpreted them as pictures of animals, mythical people, and other objects.

The planets move against a narrow background of constellations. This background is called the zodiac. This is a Greek word meaning "circle of animals." The constellations in the zodiac are Aries (the ram); Taurus (the bull); Pisces (the fish); Cancer (the crab); Leo (the lion); Scorpio (the scorpion); Sagittarius (half horse, half man); Capricorn (the goat); Gemini (the twins); Libra (the scales); Virgo (the virgin); and Aquarius (the water carrier).

These 12 constellations divide the zodiac into 12 "houses." The ancients believed these were the homes of the planet gods. Since there are 360° in a circle, each house occupies 30°. So, in Hitler's horoscope, the phrase "Sun in 29° Aries" means that the Sun seems to have the constellation of Aries "behind" it. But, in about two days' time, as the Earth continues to move around the Sun, the Sun will seem to have Taurus behind it. Astrologers say the Sun has "entered" Taurus. It will be there for about one month.

This way of measuring the movements of the planets has been used for hundreds of years. In the Middle Ages, and later, even scientists believed that astrology could predict events to come.

ADVISING THE QUEEN

One scientist who believed in astrology was John Dee. He was born in 1527, and lived until 1608.

John Dee was a respected geographer and mathematician, besides being an astrologer.

He was a brilliant English mathematician. In 1553 King Henry VIII's elder daughter, Mary, became queen of England. She was engaged to marry Philip of Spain. Dee was asked to draw up horoscopes for the couple.

Dee then met Elizabeth, Mary's half sister. He drew up her horoscope, too. He compared it with Mary's. He said that Mary would die soon, without having children. But he told Elizabeth that her future was bright. On November 17, 1558, Mary died, childless. Elizabeth was proclaimed queen.

The new queen appointed Dee as her royal astrologer. Thirty years later, in 1588, England was threatened with invasion. A huge fleet from Spain, the Armada, was approaching. Dee told the queen there would be tremendous storms. He said the Spaniards would be defeated in English waters.

On July 21 the English fleet met the Armada off the southwest coast of England. The English drove it up the Channel to Calais, France. There a gale suddenly sprang up. Forced to sail northward, the

Queen Elizabeth I's royal astrologer was John Dee. He predicted that the Spanish Armada would be destroyed by a gale. When the Armada arrived in the English Channel, a huge storm blew up.

Spaniards tried to go around the north of Scotland and the west of Ireland. But more than half the ships were wrecked. The survivors limped back to Spain.

HARD EVIDENCE

In the 17th century, the most famous astrologer was William Lilly. He began to practice astrology in 1644. Each year after that, he published an almanac of his predictions. In 1648 he forecast that the year 1665 would bring "grand catastrophe." He said it would be very bad for London. Lilly also wrote of "sundry fires and a consuming plague."

Three years later, in 1651, Lilly published two pictures that symbolized what London could expect. One showed corpses wrapped in shrouds and men digging graves. The other showed people fighting a blaz-ing fire. Overhead was a pair of twins, the zodiac sign of the Gemini. They were diving into the flames. Gemini was the astrological sign for London.

The plague that hit England in 1665 was predicted by astrologer William Lilly. He also predicted the Great Fire of London, which followed in 1666.

In 1665 there was an outbreak of bubonic plague (a disease caused by bacteria and spread by fleas) in London. People fled from the city. They carried the infection to other parts of the country. Thousands died. The following year, fire broke out in a baker's shop in Pudding Lane, in the heart of London. It spread rapidly. It destroyed most of the city center.

Lilly's prediction made him famous. But some people suspected that he might have started the fire himself to make his prediction come true! Lilly was summoned before a special committee set up by Parliament. But he managed to convince them that he was only a successful astrologer. The case against him was dropped.

PRESIDENTIAL ASTROLOGER

In recent times public figures have shown an interest in astrology. One of these was the wife of President Ronald Reagan. Nancy Reagan kept in touch regularly with the famous San Francisco astrologer Joan Quigley. She would call her with the President's schedule and ask which dates were safe and which dangerous. Then she would try to make changes, according to Quigley's advice.

When these revelations were published in the U.S. they created a public uproar. National newspapers printed sensational headlines such as "Astrologer runs the White House." But Quigley herself was quick to explain that this was not strictly the case. "An astrologer just picks the best time to do something that someone else has already planned to do. It's like being in the ocean. You should go with the waves, not against them."

"Astrologer runs the White House," shrieked the headlines. Nancy Reagan employed astrologer Joan Quigley for advice on the President's schedules.

The Hand of Fate

A popular way of telling the future is by examining the palm of a person's hand.

Louis Hamon was born in Wicklow, Ireland, in 1866. But as a palmist he called himself Cheiro. By studying the shape of a person's hand, and the lines on it, he said he could tell their character. More important, he claimed to be able to forecast their future.

Cheiro made his first visit to New York City in June 1894. Reporters from the newspaper *New York World* decided to test his powers. They showed him the palm prints of a man. The prints were those of a Dr. Meyer. He had just been arrested. The 44-year-old doctor was suspected of poisoning some of his patients. He had insured their lives for large sums of money.

Cheiro said: "Whether this man has committed one crime or 20 is not the question. He will be found out, arrested, tried, and sentenced to death. It will then be proved that, for years, he has used whatever profession he has followed to obtain money by crime.

"This man in his 44th year will pass through some sensational trial. He will be condemned to die. Yet his hands show that he will escape this fate, and live on for years—but in prison."

The palm print of murderer Dr. Meyer (opposite) that was shown to famous palmist Cheiro.

34

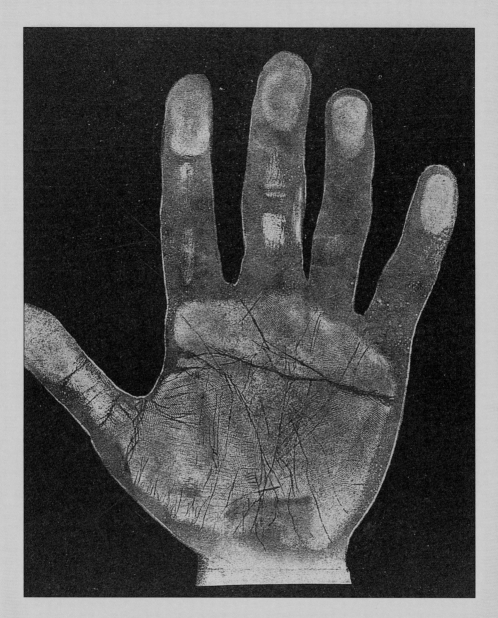

"... tell me if you stand by your words that I shall escape the chair!"

DR. MEYER

Meyer was tried and found guilty. In less than a week he was due to go to the electric chair. As a last request, he asked to be allowed to speak to Cheiro. The palmist went to the jail. The condemned man begged him, ". . . tell me if you stand by your words that I shall escape the chair!" Cheiro assured him that the Line of Life in his hand continued "clear and distinct," well past his 44th year.

"Day after day went past," Cheiro wrote. "The evening papers, full of the details of the preparations for the execution, fixed for the next morning, were eagerly brought up.

"Midnight came. Suddenly boys rushed through the streets screaming 'special edition!' I read across the front page, 'Meyer escapes the chair. Supreme Court finds flaws in the indictment.' The miracle had happened—the sentence was altered to imprisonment for life [a life sentence]. Meyer lived on for 15 years. He died peacefully in the prison hospital."

A GLITTERING FUTURE

Cheiro began his career in London, England, in 1888. He gave a consultation to a young lawyer, Edward Marshall Hall. Cheiro told him, "From 30 years of age, to the last moment of your life, your success will be steadily on the increase. You will die at the very zenith of your career." All this came to pass. Marshall Hall was the most successful defense counsel of his era when he died in 1927 at age 69.

But Cheiro said something to Hall toward the end of the meeting that was even more remarkable. "I see something vividly. I see you standing on the balcony of what looks like a large country house, with a big garden below. The grounds seem lighted up with a vivid electric light. Even the trees are lighted up with colored lamps. There are thousands of people looking up to the balcony. You are trying to speak. The faces of the crowd are very white in the strong light. Beside you is a woman waving a white handkerchief. That is what I see, but what it means is more than I can tell you."

Celebrated British lawyer Edward Marshall Hall. Cheiro told him that "From 30 years of age, to the last moment of your life, your success will be steadily on the increase."

Some time later, Marshall Hall was elected as member of Parliament for Southport, Cheshire. Before the result was announced to the waiting crowd, an election official made a request. In the past, he said, the wife of the winning candidate had waved a handkerchief in red or blue, the colors of the competing parties. This revealed the result to the crowd before it was officially announced. He said this should not be done this time.

Marshall Hall then went out onto the balcony of the town hall. His wife and the other candidates went with him. He looked down at the cheering crowd. Colored lanterns hung in the trees behind. "I've seen all this before," he thought. Then he remembered Cheiro's prophecy. He looked to his left, and saw his wife. She had taken the election official's request literally. She was waving a handkerchief at the crowd. It was neither red nor blue, but was white.

Predictions in Literature

Many writers have imagined the future, often with startling results.

Sir Francis Bacon, Lord Verulam, was an English philosopher and statesman. He lived from 1561 to 1626. He was among the first people to propose logical ways of carrying out scientific experiments. He laughed at the possibility of prediction.

Yet Francis Bacon wrote a book called *The New Atlantis*. It was published in the year of his death. In it, he imagined an ideal future world. He foresaw the telephone and the refrigerator.

Other writers, too, have imagined ideal worlds. But few—if any—of their predictions have come true. Science-fiction writers have had the greatest success.

One of the earliest science-fiction writers was the Frenchman Jules Verne. In 1865 he published *From the Earth to the Moon*. *Round the Moon* followed in 1870. Verne's spacecraft in these books was called the *Columbiad*. It was fired from Florida. It splashed down in the Pacific. The crew were rescued by a ship from the United States.

Columbiad was fitted with rockets to return from the Moon. They would also slow the craft down as it reentered Earth's atmosphere.

U.S. astronaut Buzz Aldrin walks on the moon in 1969 (opposite). French author Jules Verne had predicted this over 100 years earlier.

"Verne's spacecraft . . . was called Columbiad. It was fired from Florida."

Verne wrote that the flight from Earth to the Moon lasted 97 hours and 13 minutes. The flight time of *Apollo 11*'s trip to the Moon and back in 1969 was a total of 195 hours 18 minutes. That made an average of 97 hours 39 minutes each way.

Jules Verne wrote at a time when science and engineering were making tremendous progress. He made use of all the latest developments in his books. But he went further than the facts. He imagined many things not yet invented. In addition to space travel, he described huge submarines that could travel for days beneath the ocean. Airplanes, radio, and television also appear in his writing.

FANTASTIC IMAGININGS

In 1863 Verne wrote a book called *Paris in the 20th Century*. It described the capital of France as it would be in 100 years from his time. Silent passenger trains ran through the city. The streets were brilliantly lit by 100,000 mercury arc lights. Cars, cabs, and trucks were powered by motors that ran on hydrogen gas. Their drivers steered with a wheel, and they changed speed with a foot pedal. And everybody, said Verne, was filled with "an American urgency."

Arthur C. Clarke foresaw communications satellites.

In the banks there were calculating machines. They had keyboards "like pianos." Letters could be sent directly from one place to another via "electric telegraph." This telegraph was connected to "dials" in all the stock exchanges of the world. Documents were sent by a type of fax machine.

In the movie 2001: A Space Odyssey, *the astronauts are on a deep-space mission to Jupiter. NASA has no such plans—yet.*

British author H. G. Wells also made scientific predictions of the future. But his stories were more far-fetched than those of Jules Verne. In *The War of the Worlds*, published in 1898, he described the invasion of Earth by creatures from Mars. The flying machines he imagined were huge. Machines like them would not be built for years. *The Shape of Things to Come* was published in 1933. In it Wells warned of a destructive world war, followed by the colonization of other planets by people from Earth.

Several modern science-fiction writers have a background in technology. One of the most famous is Arthur C. Clarke. He was a radar instructor during World War II. As early as 1945, he published plans for a communications satellite. Many people thought he was crazy. But 20 years later the first communications satellite was launched. Clarke then began to write science fiction. In 1968 he worked with Stanley Kubrick on a film based on his short story "The Sentinel." This was *2001: A Space Odyssey.*

Can We See the Future?

People have different ways to explain how we can see into the future.

Is it really possible to prophesy the future? The stories told in this book would make you think it is. But these only deal with predictions that came true. Most professional prophets, psychics, and fortune-tellers have had as many—if not more—failures as successes.

MISTAKEN PROPHECIES

In early 1939 people feared war with Germany. So the magazine *Prediction* consulted a number of psychics and astrologers.

Geraldine Cummins was a famous psychic. In the February issue she declared that there would be no war in 1939. In June, R. H. Naylor, an astrologer, said, "No, Hitler will not lead Germany into war." And in the September issue, the editor confirmed that there would be no war for several years. World War II began on September 3, 1939.

Jeane Dixon forecast Soviet invasions of Iran and Palestine in the 1950s. They did not happen. In the 1960s she predicted the "ever-increasing presence of Russian submarines near the Bolivian coastline," apparently unaware that Bolivia has no coast. It is surrounded by other

"Jeane Dixon failed to predict the Challenger disaster in 1986. . . ."

South American countries. She claimed to have predicted the fire on board the *Apollo* command module in 1967 that killed three people. But Jeane Dixon failed to predict the *Challenger* disaster in 1986 that killed seven people.

Elizabeth Prophet, head of the Church Universal Triumphant, predicted the end of the world for April 23, 1990. She and 2,000 followers took shelter underground in the Rocky Mountains. April 23 passed without incident.

In 1939, famous psychic Geraldine Cummins predicted that Germany would not start a war.

There have also been many cases of people who claimed to have predicted an event—but only after it happened.

FAKES AND FALSEHOODS

On April 28, 1981, television networks broadcast a recorded interview. It was with Los Angeles psychic Tamara Rand. It was said to have been taped on March 28 in Atlanta, Georgia. That was two days before the assassination attempt on President Ronald Reagan by John Hinckley.

In the interview Tamara Rand said President Reagan would be shot in the chest by a young man. The attack would occur in the first week of April. There would be "a hail of bullets." The young man had sandy-colored hair. She said his first name was Jack. His surname was something like "Humley."

The prediction caused a sensation. But investigation revealed that it had been taped on March 31—the day after President Reagan was shot.

Richard Newton was a teacher from Gloucester, Massachusetts. He set out to show that anybody can make an accurate prediction. He claimed it does not need dreams, visions, horoscopes, or palm readings.

In December 1978, Newton appeared on television. He forecast there would be a fatal plane crash on March 11, 1979. The plane would have a red symbol on its tail. It would crash just outside a city in the Northern Hemisphere. Forty-five people would die. On March 14, 1979, a plane of Royal Jordanian Airlines crashed at Doha, Qatar, in the Persian Gulf. The death toll was 47. Not the precise date and death toll forecast by Newton, but close enough.

How did Newton do it? His explanation was that he had a book called *Destination Disaster*, which contained plane crash statistics. He discovered that most passenger planes fly in the Northern Hemisphere. Crashes usually occur on takeoff or landing. Airports

Psychic Tamara Rand claimed to have predicted the assassination attempt on President Ronald Reagan. But the "prediction" was made the day after the incident (above).

are always near cities. More than half of the world's airlines have some red in their tail symbols. And the book listed more crashes in the second week of March than at any other time. Finally, the average number killed in a crash was 45.

Richard Newton put all these facts together. He was able to figure out if such a disaster was likely to happen in the coming months.

Seers and psychics would deny this is how they work. But, subconsciously, they may pick up all kinds of ideas—even tiny hints. Then they build them into a picture. Seers and psychics claim they "see" only the finished picture. And they say this is because the future already exists. This idea has troubled thinkers for centuries. If the future is fixed, we cannot change it.

TRAVELING IN TIME

A group of physicists have recently been putting their minds to this problem. They have developed a theory that millions upon millions of universes exist, containing all possible pasts and futures. "Wormholes" may exist between these universes. It could be that psychics and other seers can see down these wormholes to future universes.

Some physicists believe that, at some time in the future, it may even be possible for humans to travel down these wormholes into another universe and reappear at some time in the past or the future.

Seer John William Dunne, who foretold the eruption of Mount Pélee in 1902, had a theory about how prediction works. He compared a person's life to a journey on a train. Sometimes it is possible to foresee a disaster a little way ahead. The person can then decide to stay on the train with its fixed future, or to jump off. This act would change the course of his or her life.

Glossary

assassin A person who murders someone for money, or for political reasons.

assassinate (vb) The action of the assassin. "He was paid to assassinate the President."

assassination (n) The name for the act of the assassin. "It was an assassination."

astrology The study of the movements of the stars and planets in relation to each other.

bubonic plague A deadly disease spread by fleas. It caused swellings, or "buboes," of the glands. In 1665, an outbreak killed thousands of people in England.

catastrophe A terrible disaster, usually involving loss of life.

command module Part of a space vehicle that can be operated as a separate, self-contained unit.

constellations The various groups of stars that have special names.

eerily Strangely, or frighteningly.

forewarning To warn of an event in advance of it actually occurring.

Führer A strong, powerful leader. Adolf Hitler was called the Führer.

indictment A written statement by a legal prosecutor that charges a person with an offense.

ominous Giving a warning that something bad is going to happen. "It was an ominous noise."

palmist A person who claims to be able to tell someone's future by "reading" the lines on their palms.

premonitions Dreams, visions, or feelings that warn of unpleasant events that are about to occur.

prophecy The foretelling of what will happen in the future. Based on feelings rather than evidence.

psychics People who claim to be able to see into the future, receive "messages" from the dead, or have other powers that cannot be scientifically explained.

seers Prophets, or people who can tell what will happen in the future.

swastika An ancient sign of a cross with each arm bent at a right angle. In the 20th century it was used as the symbol for Adolf Hitler's German Nazi Party.

visor The movable front part of a helmet.

zenith The highest point in the sky, or the greatest moment in the development of a person or thing.

zodiac An imaginary belt in space along which the Sun, Moon, and planets appear to travel. It is divided into 12 groups of stars, or constellations.

Index

Aberfan tragedy, Wales, 12, 15
air disasters, 6–8, 9–10, 45–46
Armada, Spanish, 31–32
assassinations, 8–9, 25, 44
astrology, 26–33, 42

Bacon, Sir Francis, 38
Booth, David, 6–8
Buck, Dr. Alice, 9–10

Cazotte, Jacques, 21–22
Chapman, John, 11
Cheiro, 17, 34–37
Clarke, Arthur C., 41
Cummins, Geraldine, 42, 44

de Kerlor, W., 17
Dee, John, 30–32
Dixon, Jeane, 24–25, 42–44
dream predictions, 4–11, 12–17
Dunne, John William, 10, 46

Ebertin, Elsbeth, 26, 28
election results, 24–25, 36–37

Engleton, Grace, 14–15

failed predictions, 42–44
faked predictions, 44
fire, Great Fire of London, 21, 32–33
French Revolution, 22

Godley, John, 4–6
Great Fire of London, 21, 32-33

Hall, Edward Marshall, 36-37
Henri II, King of France, 20–21
Hitler, Adolf, 24, 26, 28
horse racing results, 4–6

Jones, Eryl Mai, 12

Kennedy, President John F., 25

Lilly, William, 32–33
Lincoln, President Abraham, 8–9

Meyer, Dr., 34–36
Middleton, J. C., 15–16
Mount Pelée, 10, 46

Naylor, R. H., 42

Newton, Richard, 44–46
Nostradamus, 18–21
novels, predictions in, 17, 38–41

palmistry, 34–37
plague of 1665, 32
prophecy, 18–25, 42–44
Prophet, Elizabeth, 44

Quigley, Joan, 33

rail disasters, 10
Rand, Tamara, 44, 45
Reagan, President Ronald and Mrs. Nancy, 33, 44, 45
Robertson, Morgan, 17

science fiction, 38–41
space exploration, 38–39, 41, 44
Spanish Armada, 31–32

time travel, 46
Titanic disaster, 15–17

Verne, Jules, 38–40

Wells, H. G., 41
World War II, 21, 23–24, 28, 42

Further Reading

Asimov, Isaac. *Science Fiction: Visions of Tomorrow.* Walz-Chojnacki, Greg, rev. Gareth Stevens, 1995

Green, Carl R. and Sanford, William R. *Recalling Past Lives.* Enslow, 1993

Landau, Elaine. *Fortune Telling,* "Mysteries of Science" series. Millbrook Press, 1996

Royer, Mary P. *Astrology: Opposing Viewpoints.* "Great Mysteries" series. Greenhaven, 1991